PUNCH

ALL CREATURES
GREAT AND SMALL

First published in Great Britain in 2009 by Prion
an imprint of
The Carlton Publishing Group
20 Mortimer Street
London W1T 3JW

10 9 8 7 6 5 4 3 2 1

A catalogue record for this book is available from the British Library

ISBN 978-1-85375-716-7

Editorial Manager: Roland Hall
Design: Stephen Cary
Production: Claire Hayward

Printed in Dubai

PUNCH

ALL CREATURES GREAT AND SMALL

EDITED BY

HELEN WALASEK

PRION

INTRODUCTION

Punch's fascination with the animal kingdom began with that bête-noir of our Victorian ancestors – the misbehaving horse – a theme that continued right into the present day with Thelwell's inimitable grumpy ponies. Inevitably, though, the spark for literally thousands of cartoons over the decades was our complicated relationship with the best of man's furry, four-legged friends: the dog. Felines never came close…

Later, a Noah's Ark-ful of creatures strolled, flew and swam onto the pages of *Punch*. Accident-prone hedgehogs and suicidal lemmings inspired two of the most fertile of the fads that swept the world of the magazine's artists and cartoonists could rarely go wrong with a penguin. We've rounded up a clutch of the best, so commune with the critters with this collection of animal classics.

'I'm afraid you'll have to stop the bus – Mrs Scully needs
the lavatory again.'

7

'You've just ruined what, until now, had been
a highly successful day.'

'Curses! We're too late! He's changed into
a protected species!'

'Shall we send him, or will he take you with him?'

'We felt he could
use the exercise.'

11

'And we've virtually eliminated the possibility
of nuclear war through human error.'

'*Sorry I thought you were someone else.*'

'When **will** Rex realise that Captain
Garth-Boothby is a guest?'

'Just get on with the cleaning out, O'Shea – no need to rub their noses in it.'

'*Come on Gordon! The Japanese evening was your idea.*
How do I get the little bastard to let go of the plate?'

'He's having problems with the motions.'

17

'Gee, honey... Warfarin! Smells good!'

'*Oh go on – I made the breakfast last year.*'

20

BREAKING IN
PLEASE PASS

21

The Litigious Rodent

'Jake b'lieves in letting sleeping dawgs lie!'

'And old friend of yours has dropped
by to cheer you up.'

'I thought Norman had been looking
a bit depressed lately.'

Owner of dog *(to timid stranger).* '*Just give him
a good whack and send him here.*'

'You're quite right – all that huffing and puffing does seem to have caused a certain amount of structural damage, but as it comes under acts of terrorism, I'm afraid it won't be covered by your insurance policy.'

'You'll never regret this – he was a pretty dumb parrot.'

'Other women? What other women?'

'Why wait till Father's Day?
Give it to him now.'

Tar-rahhh!!

'*Shall we lead them astray?*'

RODIN'S
JACK RUSSELL

34

'We ought to buy a bigger catflap, darling.'

'But you had a fiver only last week.'

'These lights seem to be taking
a long time to change.'

'Excuse me son – just what sort of bird ringing did you do on your youth training scheme?'

'And another thing, when was the last time any of us was invited to dine at the Captain's table?'

'*I'm fairly philosophical about being boiled.*
What I object to is being dressed.'

40

Mistress. *'You must have heard Fido fall downstairs, Emily,
and you never came down to see if he'd hurt himself.'*
Emily. *'Good gracious! I thought it was you, mum.'*

41

'Hamster migration – every seven years.'

'Still, it must have been over quite quickly.'

43

'Give me a fag, any day!'

'Son... Son?'

'I don't do bridge work for under £200.'

'Stop criticizing.'

*'It's your flaming mother again. She says
I'm not giving you enough bananas.'*

'It's spring all right – the tortoise is awake!'

51

'He's got more money than sense.'

'Hello, Sainsbury's? Do you sell dog food for very naughty puppies? No? Well, I certainly don't blame you. Thank you, Sainsbury's and goodbye.'

'The only thing your father ever
gave me was indigestion.'

'May the Lord bless the reading of
His holy word and this cat.'

'Can I get him to ring you back?
He's trying to out-stare the dog again.'

'Oh shut up.'

'I'm sorry, son, but it was kinder to put
your lemming out of its misery.'

59

'First the sign language. Then the knife and fork.
Then the toothbrush. Don't you ever know when to stop?'

'Yes, sir, we try our best to keep
them in their natural habitat.'

'Nothing personal, Pooh, but we figured you'd
fetch a fortune on the open market.'

'Merciful heavens, Winston!
Where did you learn to tango like that?'

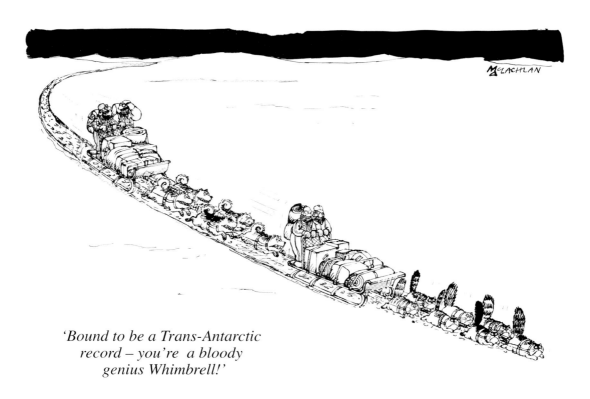

*'Bound to be a Trans-Antarctic
record – you're a bloody
genius Whimbrell!'*

'No, really, the tap-dance makes a fine finale –
don't bother about the striptease.'

'The lambs seem very subdued this year.'

'I appreciate you've changed your mind about
having children but I'm afraid these operations
are irreversible in practically all cases.'

'Yeah, I'm a rhinoceros, so what? Jesus! Why do people always
have to categorise each other?'

'Hi there – I'm the Entertainments Director around here.'

'*You always get a few troublemakers in any flock.*'

'If there's one thing worse than being in a zoo,
it's being in a children's zoo.'

'It's at about seventy I get this funny knocking noise.'

THE TALE OF SANDY

5.

6.

Daily Mirror

MUST SANDY DIE?

HOMELESS WAIF THAT NOBODY LOVES

7.

8.

9.

10.

11.

12.

'Relax – it's one of ours!'

81

'Are you sure Togo is tied to the tree, darling? I thought
I heard him running about.'
'Er – he's still tied to the tree, dear.'

'*What do you mean, no?*'

83

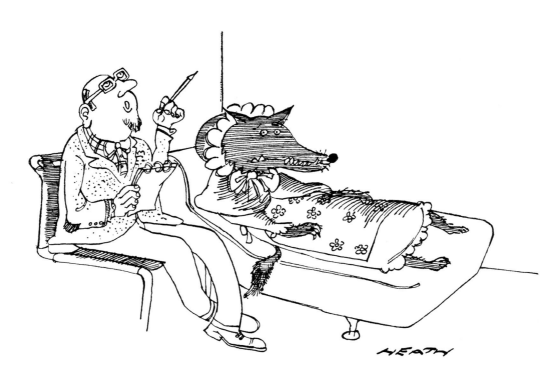

'When did you first feel the need to wear women's clothing?'

'It beats the hell out of mazes – you just make
each side a different colour, and they throw
you a piece of cheese.'

'I must say he's unusually small –
even for a chihuahua.'

'*Actually, I'm standing on a Russian submarine.*'

'I told you not to let him sense your fear.'

'*Nibbles (Hamster Raving Loony), 17,531*'

'I've been looking all over for you.'

'I don't know... it was there when I woke up this morning...'

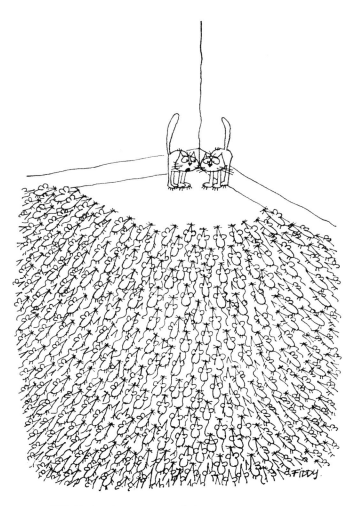

'*Well don't just stand there – negotiate!*'

'*Some terrific idea of yours – migrating to Japan.*'

'Hello, RSPCA?'

99

'It's a worm – don't get taken in by the disguise.'

'It's a little chilly, so I've put
an extra dog on your bed.'

'I love you if you're female.'

'Until finally just his hairball remains.'

*'Well, as a matter of fact we call it
"Aunt Evelyn," Aunt Evelyn.'*

BANX

106

'Elephants Graveyard, please. Single.'

'Well, I've been in three or four documentaries,
two feature films and loads of commercials,
of course. Mostly as a dog.'

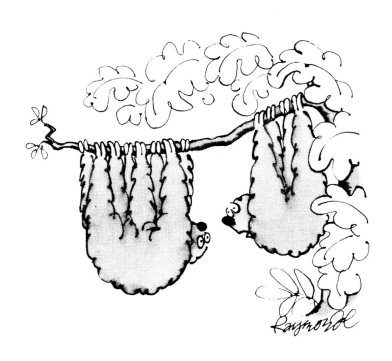

'Admit it Julian – there's
someone else, isn't there?'

'As our pets are not taking their holiday with us, Hawkins,
I have changed them round as a little treat.'

111

*'I take it you've never been to one of Lassie's wild
Hollywood parties before.'*

'Poor Eric, he'd got to within two yards
of the princess when her private
detective stamped on him.'

*'I thought we might as well get rid of a few
head lice while we're here.'*

'It took time but we finally got him house-trained.'

'We'll pay for this tomorrow.'

GIOVANNETTI

117

THE BRITISH CHARACTER
Interest in natural history

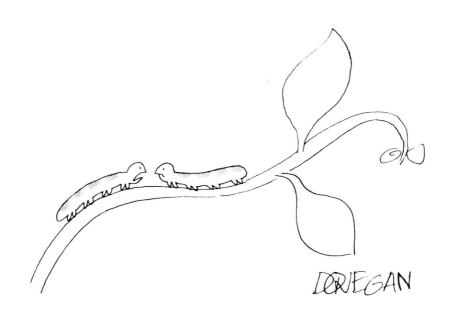

'You know what worries me?
I've never seen an old caterpillar.'

'Ten to one the dog's dug up
Mrs Perkins's geraniums again.'

'I know that cat's done something in
here – I can smell it.'

'Frankly, what attracted me to Sylvia in the first place was the prospect of some really kinky sex. Of course, that was replaced with a deep and abiding mutual love.'

'And this is playful little "Pepe" as he was when we
found him wandering the Spanish back streets.'

'...had a sheep dip last night and I can't do a thing with it.'

'I'm leaving her all my internal
organs in my will.'

'I'll serve the parrot, but the rest of you are drunk!'

'I was wondering if you had a piece of hooked wire or
something – I seem to have locked myself out.'

*'But you **are** my best friend. There's no
need to sign our names in blood.'*

*'This will be the tenth time I've bailed out
and it doesn't even look like rain yet!'*

'I still say he must have belonged to somebody.'

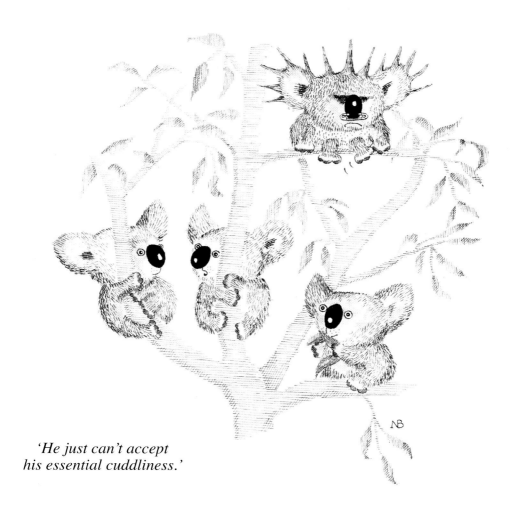

*'He just can't accept
his essential cuddliness.'*

135

'And here's one of me and the wife at Margate.'

'Could you spare a minute, Mr. Wainwright?'

'Right, which one is the boil?'

'Here he comes –
I bet he's forgotten the cigarettes.'

'He's such a snob he's changed his name to Escargot.'

'Of course it's only a gerbil substitute, really.'

*'For the last time! I will not have him inside this
house until you've done your homework.'*

'*Margaret thinks it makes him look dependable.*'

'So we said, "To hell with fish for once,
let's have an Italian".'

*'How would you like a small part in
"Macbeth", this guy said.'*

148

'There's no point fooling
ourselves – we **could** be colour-blind.'

'*Perhaps he wants to go out.*'

'Shucks, Miss Maybelle, I don't know nothin'
about women. All I know about is horses.'

'Turn that thing down. I'm trying to sleep.'

KEVIN
WOODCOCK

153

*'Look, since we're all stranded on this ice floe,
couldn't we at least be a little less formal-like
on a first name basis? I'm Chuck.'*

'Okay, what about tuna fish? Nod once if you
don't like it, nod twice if you do?'

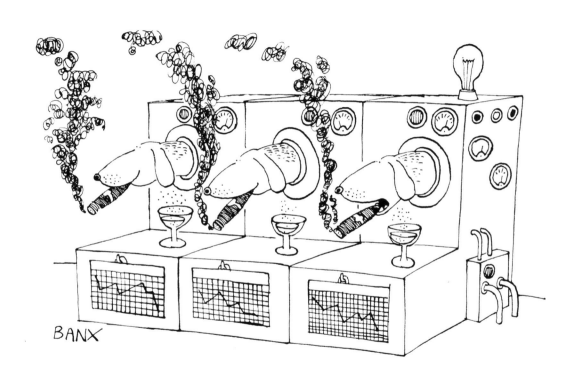

'I still say there's got to be a catch somewhere.'

'*Feed your fish, Harry. Feed your fish, Harry. Did you feed your fish, Harry? Harry, feed your fish...*'

INDEX

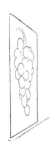

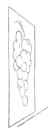

INDEX

You can purchase archive quality prints of any of the cartoons in this book.
For further information contact: Punch Cartoon Library, 87–135 Brompton Road,
London SW1 7XL, UK; telephone: +44 (0)20 7225-6710;
email: punch.library@harrods.com; www.punch.co.uk